When I Am Gloomy

わたしが しょんぼりするとき

Sam Sagolski
Illustrated by Daria Smyslova

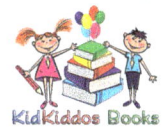

www.kidkiddos.com
Copyright ©2025 by KidKiddos Books Ltd.
support@kidkiddos.com

All rights reserved. No part of this book may be reproduced in any form or by any electronic or mechanical means, including information storage and retrieval systems, without written permission from the publisher, except in the case of a reviewer, who may quote brief passages embodied in critical articles or in a review.
First edition, 2025

Translated from English by Rina Hirai
翻訳：平井里奈

Library and Archives Canada Cataloguing in Publication
When I Am Gloomy (English Japanese Bilingual edition)/Shelley Admont
ISBN: 978-1-0497-0061-8 paperback
ISBN: 978-1-0497-0062-5 hardcover
ISBN: 978-1-0497-0063-2 eBook

Please note that the English and Japanese versions of the story have been written to be as close as possible. However, in some cases they differ in order to accommodate nuances and fluidity of each language.

One cloudy morning, I woke up feeling gloomy.
あるくもりのあさ、わたしはしょんぼりしたきもちでめをさましました。

I got out of bed, wrapped myself in my favorite blanket, and walked into the living room.
ベッドからでると、おきにいりのブランケットにくるまって、リビングへあるいていきました。

"Mommy!" I called. "I'm in a bad mood."
「ママ！」わたしはよびました。「きもちがしょんぼりしてるの。」

Mom looked up from her book. "Bad? Why do you say that, darling?" she asked.
ママは、ほんからかおをあげました。「しょんぼり？どうして？」とたずねました。

"Look at my face!" I said, pointing to my furrowed brows. Mom smiled gently.
「みて！わたしのかお！」わたしは、じぶんのしかめっつらをゆびさしながらいいました。ママはやさしくほほえみました。

"I don't have a happy face today," I mumbled. "Do you still love me when I'm gloomy?"
「きょうはしあわせなおかおじゃない。」わたしは、ぼそぼそといいました。「わたしがしょんぼりしてても、ママはわたしのことすき？」

"Of course I do," Mom said. "When you're gloomy, I want to be close to you, give you a big hug, and cheer you up."
「もちろんだよ！」ママはいいました。「あなたがしょんぼりしてるとき、ママはあなたのそばにいて、ぎゅーってして、げんきをあげたいよ。」

That made me feel a little better, but only for a second, because then I started thinking about all my other moods.
ちょっとげんきがでたけど、それはほんのいっしゅんだった。だって、ほかのいろいろなきもちのことをかんがえはじめちゃったから。

"So... do you still love me when I'm angry?"
「そしたら…わたしがおこっているときも、わたしのことすき？」

Mom smiled again. "Of course I do!"
ママはまたわらって、「もちろんだよ！」といいました。

"Are you sure?"
I asked, crossing my arms.
「ほんとうに？」
わたしはうでをくみながらききました。

"Even when you're mad, I'm still your mom. And I love you just the same."

「あなたがおこっているときでも、わたしはあなたのママだよ。そして、いつもとおなじようにあなたがだいすきだよ。」

I took a big breath. "What about when I'm shy?" I whispered.

わたしは、おおきくいきをすいました。
「じゃあわたしがはずかしがりやのときは？」とささやきました。

"I love you when you're shy too," she said. "Remember when you hid behind me and didn't want to talk to the new neighbor?"

「はずかしがりやのときも、だいすきだよ。」とママはいいました。「おぼえてる？あたらしいきんじょのひととはなしたくなくて、ママのうしろにかくれてたでしょう？」

I nodded. I remembered it well.

わたしはうなずきました。そのときのことはよくおぼえていました。

"And then you said hello and made a new friend. I was so proud of you."

「それから、あなたはこんにちはっていって、あたらしいおともだちができたね。ママはとってもほこりにおもったよ。」

"Do you still love me when I ask too many questions?"
I continued.

「わたしがたくさんしつもんしても、わたしのことすき？」わたしはつづけました。

"When you ask a lot of questions, like now, I get to watch you learn new things that make you smarter and stronger every day," Mom answered. "And yes, I still love you."

「いまみたいに、たくさんのしつもんをするとね、ママはあなたがまいにちすこしずつかしこく、つよくなっていくのをみられるんだよ。」とママはこたえました。

「もちろん、ママはいつだってあなたのことがだいすきだよ。」

"What if I don't feel like talking at all?" I continued asking.
「もしわたしがぜんぜんおはなししたくないときはどうするの？」と、わたしはたずねつづけました。

"Come here," she said. I climbed into her lap and rested my head on her shoulder.
「こっちにおいで。」とママがいいました。
わたしはママのひざにのり、かたにもたれました。

"When you don't feel like talking and just want to be quiet, you start using your imagination. I love seeing what you create," Mom answered.

「おはなししたくなくて、ただしずかにしていたいときはね、そうぞうりょくをつかってごらん。ママは、あなたがなにかをつくりだすのをみるのがだいすきなんだ。」とママはこたえました。

Then she whispered in my ear, "I love you when you're quiet too."

「しずかなあなたもだいすきだよ。」ママはみみもとで、ささやきました。

"But do you still love me when I'm afraid?" I asked.

「でも、わたしがこわがっているときは、わたしのことすき？」わたしはたずねました。

"Always," said Mom. "When you're scared, I help you check that there are no monsters under the bed or in the closet."

「いつもすきだよ。」ママはいいました。「あなたがこわがっているとき、モンスターがベッドのしたやクローゼットにいないか、たしかめるよ。」

She kissed me on the forehead. "You are so brave, my sweetheart."

ママはわたしのおでこにキスをしました。「あなたはとってもゆうきがある、わたしのかわいいこよ。」

"And when you're tired," she added softly, "I cover you with your blanket, bring you your teddy bear, and sing you our special song."
　「それから、つかれたときはね」とママはやさしくいいました。「ブランケットをかけて、テディベアをもってきて、わたしたちのとくべつなうたをうたってあげるよ。」

"What if I have too much energy?" I asked, jumping to my feet.

「もしげんきがありあまっていたら？」と、わたしはとびおきて、ききました。

She laughed. "When you're full of energy, we go biking, skip rope, or run around outside together. I love doing all those things with you!"

ママはわらいました。「げんきいっぱいのときは、いっしょにじてんしゃにのったり、なわとびをしたり、そとではしったりするんだよ。そういうことをあなたとするのが、ママはだいすきなんだ！」

"But do you love me when I don't want to eat broccoli?" I stuck out my tongue.

「ブロッコリーをたべたくないときも、わたしのことすき？」わたしはしたをぺろっとだしました。

Mom chuckled. "Like that time you slipped your broccoli to Max? He liked it a lot."

ママはくすくすわらいました。「あのときブロッコリーをマックスにこっそりあげたでしょ？マックスはとってもよろこんでいたよ。」

"You saw that?" I asked.
「みてたの?」とわたしはたずねました。

"Of course I did. And I still love you, even then."
「もちろんみてたよ。それでもママはいつだって、あなたのことがだいすきだよ。」

I thought for a moment, then asked one last question:
わたしはすこしかんがえて、さいごのしつもんをしました。

"Mommy, if you love me when I'm gloomy or mad... do you still love me when I'm happy?"
「ねぇママ、もしわたしがしょんぼりしているときや、おこっているときもだいすきなら…わたしがうれしいときも、だいすき？」

"Oh, sweetheart," she said, hugging me again, "when you're happy, I'm happy too."
「まあ、かわいいこ。」とママはまたぎゅっとだきしめながら、いいました。
「あなたがうれしいときは、ママもうれしいんだよ。」

She kissed me on the forehead and added, "I love you when you're happy just as much as I love you when you're sad, or mad, or shy, or tired."
ママはわたしのおでこにキスをして、「あなたがうれしいときも、かなしいときも、おこっているときも、はずかしがっているときも、つかれているときも、ママはあなたのことがだいすきだよ。」

I snuggled close and smiled. "So... you love me all the time?" I asked.

わたしはママにぴったりくっついて、にっこりわらいました。「じゃあ…いつでもわたしのことがだいすきってこと？」とききました。

"All the time," she said. "Every mood, every day, I love you always."

「いつでも。」とママはいいました。「どんなきもちでも、まいにち、いつもだいすきだよ。」

As she spoke, I started feeling something warm in my heart.
ママのことばをきいて、わたしのこころはあたたかくなりました。

I looked outside and saw the clouds floating away. The sky was turning blue, and the sun came out.
そとをみると、くもがながれていくのがみえました。そらがあおくなり、たいようがかおをだしました。

It looked like it was going to be a beautiful day after all.
どうやら、きょうはやっぱりすてきないちにちになりそうです。

www.ingramcontent.com/pod-product-compliance
Lightning Source LLC
LaVergne TN
LVHW072108060526
838200LV00061B/4832